£6.50

STEWART WILLIAMS'
CARDIFF
YESTERDAY
No.20

Endpapers: Supermarkets have revolutionised our shopping habits, but many of us still hanker after the old days of the little corner shop like this one in Atlas Place, Canton, which opened all hours to serve the local community. The Hurley family ran their business from the early years of the century until the late 1920s

1 South front of the old Central Library with the sculptured bust of Minerva looking out on the Hayes as it was in 1920. The original library building, designed by James, Seward and Thomas, was opened by Mayor Alfred Thomas (later Lord Pontypridd) in 1882. The much abused statue of John Batchelor, 'The Friend of Freedom', has been moved a few yards and now stands in the centre of a roundabout in the new road lay-out, while the Hayes Island snack bar was at that time a tramway parcels office. From there parcels were delivered to all parts of the city by messengers. It was closed in 1939

STEWART WILLIAMS'
CARDIFF
YESTERDAY
No. 20

Foreword by
Ernie Curtis

Historical Note by
Geoff Dart

Soccer Profile by
Richard Shepherd
BBC Radio Wales Football Commentator

First published April, 1989

© Stewart Williams, Publishers,
1 Trem-y-Don, Barry, South Glamorgan

ISBN 1 870402 30 8

ACKNOWLEDGEMENTS

Warm thanks are extended to the following individuals and organisations whose photographs appear in this volume:—

Arthur Atkins 103, 104, 105, 106, 107, 175; Mrs Clarice Atkins 121, 122, 188, 190; Mrs Patricia Bird 97; Mrs L. Bolt 86, 207; Mrs Doris Brown 101, 102; Dick Cooke 145, 146; Miss Beryl Coombs 132; Mrs E. Crean 91, 136; A. V. Dadd 166, 174, 193, 195, 197; Mrs E. Danks 152, 153, 154; Mrs Margaret Dart 162; Mrs M. Denning 78, 92, 168, 169; Mrs B. Dunscombe 84, 112, 113, 114, 131, 177, 178; Brian Edwards 163; Norman Escott 98; George C. Evans 185; Leslie Farr 161; Albert Harcom 56, 57; C. W. Hill 209; Mrs Muriel Hooper 118; Mr & Mrs A. J. Ions 47, 80, 82, 128, 138, 165; Mrs S. James 137; Stan James 108, 109; Fred Jones *endpapers*, 4, 5, 18, 19, 20, 21, 22, 29, 30, 31, 33, 34, 38, 39, 40, 42, 43, 45, 46, 54, 55, 58, 60, 62, 71, 72, 129, 143, 155, 179, 180, 181, 182, 183, 184, 206, 211; A. J. W. Keir 37, 77; Mrs F. M. Kelleher 48, 81, 120; Mrs Thelma Lusty 156, 157, 158; Mrs Irene Moss 127, 176; W. J. O'Neill 210; Mrs Myra Page 83, 119, 133, 134, 135, 172, 189; Stan Parker 28; Leonard Passmore 79, 167, 173; Tom Paul 159, 160; W. Penney 11, 12, 13, 14, 15, 16, 110, 111; Tom Phillips 44; Reg Potter 170; J. M. Prickett 49, 50, 51; Mrs C. P. Priest 89, 90; Terry Rees 94, 100, 115, 116, 151, 192, 212; Norman J. Rich 123, 124, 125, 126, 130, 144; Mrs E. Richards 117, 171, 194; South Glamorgan Public Libraries 3, 6, 7, 8, 9, 10, 23, 24, 25, 26, 27, 73, 75, 76, 99, 191, 198, 199, 200, 201, 202, 203, 204; *South Wales Echo* 63, 64, 65, 66, 67, 68, 69, 70; Rev. Bryan Snaith 87, 88, 95, 96, 139, 140, 141, 142, 205; Bert Street 85; Alf Townsend 32, 41, 52, 53, 208; Miss Barbara Treble 147, 148, 149, 150; Robert Williams 74; Stewart Williams 1, 2, 17, 35, 36, 59, 61; Mrs W. Wiltshire 196; Mrs Win Witcomb 93, 164, 186, 187

Printed in Wales by D. Brown & Sons Ltd., Cowbridge and Bridgend, Glamorgan

Foreword

by ERNIE CURTIS

last surviving member of the Cardiff City side
who won the FA Cup in 1927

When people ask me what I think of present day soccer I tell them that in my opinion it does not begin to compare with the old days. You see, I was lucky enough to be in the game long before big money took away most of the magic. I was born in Lansdowne Road, Canton, in 1907 and was playing for my school, Severn Road, at eight years of age. The school was a nursery of talent—it provided eight of the Cardiff Boys' team that won the English Schools' Shield for the first time. In those days it was every boy's ambition to become a soccer star and many hours were spent developing skills, often playing with a tennis ball for hours on end until control was mastered. After playing amateur soccer for Severn Road Old Boys in the local leagues, I was invited to join Cardiff City in 1925, still as an amateur, whilst continuing to work as an apprentice electrician for the Corporation. But it was not long before a full-time contract was offered to me by manager Fred Stewart and I made my first team debut against Manchester United in September 1926. This was the start of my professional involvement with the game which has lasted, on and off, for over 60 years.

The highspot came early in my career—having the great good fortune to be chosen to play for the City against Arsenal in the 1927 FA Cup Final at Wembley and returning home with a cup winner's medal. Although it took place so long ago the memories are still vivid. It was an occasion that could have bowled over a 19-year-old, but in the dressing room our captain Fred Keenor rolled up his sleeves and said 'Let's get out there, fight and win. Let's get to it lads!' And that was all we needed, although surprisingly enough I had no trace of pre-match nerves. Not even when Fred Keenor introduced me to King George V. He shook my hand and mumbled a few words which I did not take in. Friends asked me afterwards what he said and I told them, 'Hello Ernie, how are you?' 'Fine George, see you after the game.' But joking apart, it was a great honour. Our 1-0 victory made soccer history—bringing the trophy home to Wales for the first and only time. I have never known such excitement. The celebrations began at the stadium and continued at our banquet in the Palace Hotel, Bloomsbury, where the entire floor of the dining room was carpeted in artificial grass to make it look like the Wembley pitch. Our homecoming was delayed until the Monday to give the city time to prepare—and also the stations down the line from Paddington. Every one was decked out in blue and white in our honour. Then to a welcome I shall never forget. Over 250,000 packed the centre of Cardiff to see us arrive at the station and then drive to the City Hall for the civic reception. It was the most moving occasion of my life, the stuff of dreams, and I shall always bless my good fortune.

Ernie Curtis

Historical Note

Photographs 54 and 55 recall Cardiff General (now Central) station in the heyday of the Great Western Railway some sixty years ago. Soon it was to be rebuilt together with the introduction of electric colour-light signalling and extensive permanent way engineering work involving the main line from Newtown to Ely Bridge. The project commenced in 1930 and was completed early in 1934; its complexity was such that the *G.W.R. Magazine* for March 1934 took 19 pages to describe and illustrate it in detail. A major element comprised the diversion of the ground-level main line on to an embankment from Canton to Ely Bridge including the construction of bridges at Leckwith Road and Sanatorium Road. These replaced two notorious level crossings; one gave access to the Sanatorium from Canton and the other, known to railwaymen as Canton Crossing, obstructed Leckwith Road. In common with many in the crowds which flocked to Ninian Park on Saturday afternoons, I found the large gates of the latter extremely frustrating because they always seemed to shut when the kick-off was imminent. The old General was an open station, no tickets being required to enter it; this was a great bonus for my companions and me in our locomotive-spotting days which coincided with the rebuilding period. It could irritate incoming passengers, however, because trains were delayed at the penultimate stop while Cardiff tickets were collected. I still retain childhood memories of long trains, packed with families tired after a long day at the seaside, held for what could seem like ages at Grangetown Station while a small army of ticket collectors worked their way along the compartments. This operation became part of Cardiff Yesterday on 26 February 1934 when, as the *Railway Magazine* reported in its issue for April, Cardiff General had ceased to be the last open station in South Wales and that this would avoid the collection of Cardiff tickets at Newport, Marshfield, Ely and elsewhere. Almost 55 years later, however, the *South Wales Echo* was able to report on 4 January 1989 that British Rail management believed that the Open Station System, which had come into operation that week at the largest station in South Wales, was already being appreciated by passengers who were no longer delayed at barriers.

No doubt readers of this series will also appreciate a rare, if not unique, example of Cardiff To-day reverting to Cardiff Yesterday!

GEOFF DART

Author's Note

Setting publishing targets is always risky. My original projection of a ten volume *Cardiff Yesterday* series was thought by many, myself included, to be rather more optimistic than realistic. Yet here we are, with barely a pause for breath, at No. 20 having doubled the target figure. The satisfaction this gives is immense and to know the books give great pleasure to many thousands of Cardiffians is an added bonus. Memories galore have been rekindled by the seemingly endless stream of photographs, submitted from far and wide, which have reflected so many aspects of city life down the years.

I have always stressed that the series is the result of teamwork, so as we reach this milestone it seems a good time to set on record once again my sincere thanks to those whose 'dedication to the cause' matches my own. Geoff Dart, former County Librarian of South Glamorgan, must head the list. From the outset he has given unstinting support, making available his unique knowledge of the city's history and always being on hand to help and advise; then there are other old friends like John F. Andrews, Bill Barrett, Dick Cooke, Bill Coombes, Viv Corbin, Ken Goode, Bill and Dennis O'Neill, Bill Penney, and Richard Shepherd who have helped in many ways. A special word of thanks also to my son, Robert, who has provided some excellent maps and photographs. As the acknowledgements show, hundreds of kind people have sent me photographs, but the majority have come from Fred Jones of Rumney and from South Glamorgan County Libraries. I am deeply grateful to them.

Many have discovered the books through the serialisations in the *South Wales Echo* and I am indebted to the editor, my good friend Geoff Rich, for his backing and also for his advice which has always been sound. Lastly a few lines of appreciation to my printers, D. Brown & Sons Ltd, and in particular Bob Whitaker for producing the end-products; Pete Makin of Scanagraphics Ltd, East Moors, and his cameraman Andy Wassall for expertly processing the photographs, and the Western Book Company for binding the job, the final operation before *Cardiff Yesterday* reaches the bookshops.

STEWART WILLIAMS

City, Suburbs and Docks

2 Open-top trams rattle along the Hayes, their passengers enjoying the sunny morning in 1912. Except for one 'bay' of the former Noah Rees building the right-hand side of the photograph has been totally transformed since the Second World War

3 This was the city centre in June 1930. The Fish Market stood on the corner site in the Hayes, now the SWEB showrooms; James Howell's award-winning building on the corner of St. Mary Street and Wharton Street was under construction; Greyfriars Road had just been built, and the Arms Park was still a modest arena

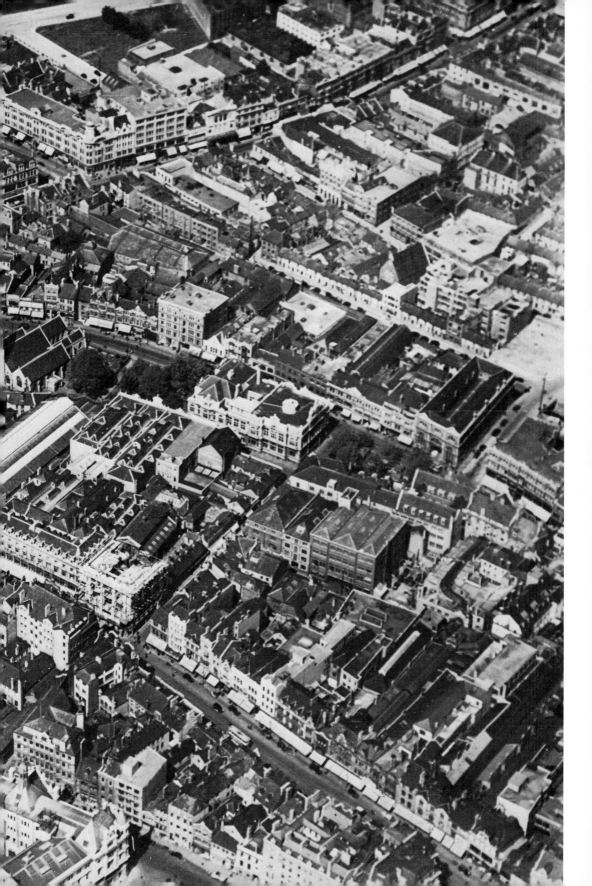

University College, Cardiff.

NATIONAL PAGEANT OF WALES. CARDIFF.
JULY 26 TO AUG 7 1909

RHWYSG HANES CYMRU.
THRILLING EPISODES.
HISTORIC COSTUMES.
GREAT NATIONAL SPECTACLE.

Y DDRAIG GOCH DDYRY GYCHWYN

4/5 The former Glamorgan and Monmouthshire Infirmary in Newport Road, first home of the University College of South Wales & Monmouthshire in 1883 when the Infirmary moved to Longcross. It was demolished in 1960. No difficulty in dating this photograph—the hoarding fixed to the railings carries the poster *left* advertising the National Pageant of Wales which was held in Cardiff from 26 July to 7 August 1909

6 Rhymney Railway passenger terminus 'Cardiff (The Parade)' seen from the air in 1927. It was closed in the following year. The coal sidings at Senghennydd Road are full of wagons—and see the open spaces in Cathays Park, now the site of the Welsh Office, Temple of Peace, new Police HQ, Museum and University extensions

7 Cardiff Royal Infirmary dominates this 1930 view. The Institute for the Blind building on the corner of Longcross Street was destroyed by enemy action in the Second World War and Graham Buildings opposite Roath Library in Newport Road had just been built

8 Queen Street from the air in 1927. Work had started on Greyfriars Road which was opened in the following year; on the right hand edge the huge bulk of the 5-year-old Capitol is prominent; in the foreground the Glamorganshire Canal emerges from the Tunnel into a Hill's Terrace of small, working-class houses, soon to be demolished

9 Queen Street, *c.*1915. Principality Buildings and the Carlton Restaurant were built in 1914

10 Colonial Buildings in New Street (the Glamorganshire Canal is in the foreground) was occupied by Percy Cadle, tobacco and cigarette manufacturers, in the early 1900s, and was used by fruit and vegetable merchants when this was taken *c.*1914 with an 'artist's impression' of suggested railings which it was thought would improve the site. Twelve years later it was destroyed along with a large part of Custom House Street and New Street in one of the largest fires seen in Cardiff

11 Tunnel Court, with the *Tivoli* on the left and the Northern Raincoat shop (previously Masters) on the right, prior to their demolition in 1960 to make way for the Queen's Court development. The upstairs lounge in the *Tivoli* was known world-wide to merchant seamen as the 'top-deck'

12 Taken at the same time (June 1957) the filled-in remains of the Glamorganshire Canal which ran through the heart of the city on its way to the Docks. On the left is the rear of Working Street, while right is Hill's Terrace. The warehouses were built in the late 1920s and demolished 1977-78

13 Bridge Street, looking east, as it was in 1972. The premises on the right were demolished in the early 1980s. Multi-storey car parks now occupy both sides of a much widened street

14 Oxford House and Arcade had recently been built *c.*1961-63 and the days of the old *British Volunteer*, home of the well-known Dancer family, were numbered when this was taken in 1965. Soon Hayes House and shops on the right side of Oxford Arcade would complete the transformation of the Hayes

15/16 *Above* Stealey's off-licence on the corner of Union Street and Little Union Street seen in 1956. Until the 1890s it was a pub, the *Earl of Windsor*; *left* Frank Cox's bakery in Union Street photographed at the same time. Despite the modest premises Frank enjoyed a high reputation, especially for his wedding cakes. The premises were originally occupied by the Glamorgan and Monmouthshire Dispensary before the first Infirmary was built, and remained in the ownership of Cardiff Royal Infirmary until 1957. The area was redeveloped in the 1960s and 70s

17 The housing pioneers who in 1911 promoted a company to plan and develop a garden suburb at Rhiwbina would be pleased to find it still retains a 'village' atmosphere. This is how Heol-y-Deri looked *c*.1921

18 'Peace and Plenty', after four years of war, must have seemed an attractive prospect to those early Rhiwbina settlers. This post card was postally used in 1923

19 Heoldon, Whitchurch, was built up from *c.*1905, although a road had been in existence for centuries. Taken *c.*1920

20 Three Arches viaduct over the Heath Gap was constructed during the building of the Rhymney Railway direct line via Caerphilly Tunnel 1866-71. The present Heathwood Road veers to the left and ascends on the far side of the middle arch. The low walls either side of the arches are still in situ as is the coping and parapet of the Llanishen brook culvert where it emerges from under the present Heath Halt Road. Taken in 1904

21 These houses, Nos. 1-15 Fairoak Road (part of a block that extends to Wedal Road) date from *c.*1900. The Rhymney Railway bridge, banned to drivers of double-deck 'buses and tall vehicles, has nevertheless been the undoing of many who were fooled by the rise in the road which creates an optical illusion of height. Famous novelist Eric Linklater lived in No. 23 from about 1909-13

22 Richmond Road was developed in the late 1870s and early 80s by landowner C. H. Williams of Roath Court. This traffic-free 1905 view shows Northcote Street on the right

23/24 William Booth took these photographs between 1890-92 when the 'new' Roath Park was about to dramatically alter the landscape. *Above* Looking south, this pathway ran roughly in a line from the present day Highfield Road, across Windermere Avenue to Lake Road West. The open space in the centre was soon to become the Lake botanical gardens; *below* cutting a shelf into the hillside to form the line of Lake Road East in the vicinity of the Lake promenade

25/26 *Above* The Fairoak (now reduced to a stump at the corner of the gardens). In the foreground is the bed of Tydraw Road with a pathway fenced to the railway embankment; *below* 'Gipsy camp in the new park' wrote Booth. This view, looking east, is today bounded by Wedal Road, Fairoak Road and the Rhymney Railway line (not in view); it is now roughly the site of the row of large houses and their gardens bordering the Fairoak roundabout. The thatched cottage 'Cyndda' stood at the apex of the present Shirley and Fairoak Roads

27   Rumney Court, once the home of wholesale potato importer Richard England, is now a Royal British Legion Club

28   Since the early 1930s when it was known as the Blue Horizon Club St. Mellons Country Club, with several changes of name, has catered for dancers and diners from Cardiff. The house was originally Llwynarthan, the home of Franklen G. Evans, an eminent physician, who died in 1904. It was afterwards occupied by Sir Henry Webb, Bt., Junior Lord of the Treasury and coal-owner, who converted it into an auxiliary military hospital during the First World War

ST. MELONS COUNTRY CLUB FROM
THE DRIVE, CASTLETON (GLAM).
Copyright.
CSTW. 7
Raphael Tuck & Sons, Ltd.
London.

29 St. Mellons village in 1913 seen from the height in front of the Church door. Bethania Chapel, a listed building, is seen top right

30 Castleton village from the same period. Motorists travelling between Cardiff and Newport will remember the notorious bottle-neck and hump which was only relieved when the houses *right* were demolished in the early 1960s and replaced by the small length of dual carriageway. The *Coach & Horses*, now much altered, continues to attract customers

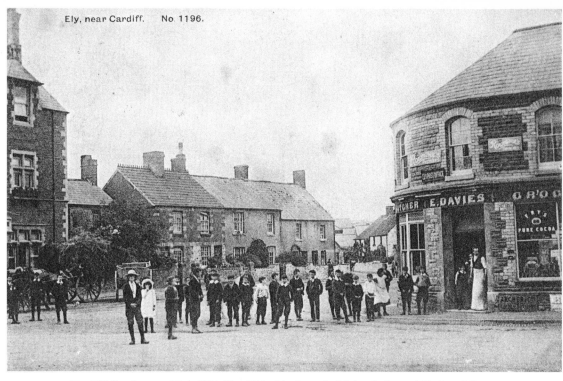

31   Mill Road corner, Ely, *c.*1906. The *White Lion* is on the left hand edge and Ely Post Office on the right

32   Bridge Road with, in the centre, the *Cow and Snuffers* which had been rebuilt in 1905. 'Yard' became 'North' *c.*1910

The Square, Llandaff Yard, Glam. No. 1325.

33 A sunny afternoon in 1907 and two young girls gather daisies in a field adjoining Whitchurch Road on which twenty years later St. Joseph's RC School would be built. In the centre is the Forward Movement Mission Hall (now Heath Evangelical Church) which had been opened in April of the previous year

34 With a view looking out towards Penarth Head and the Bristol Channel beyond, Windsor Esplanade was a very desirable place to live in 1912

Lock Gates, Bute Docks. 278.

35 Bute East Dock was a hive of activity in the years before the First World War. The tall ships *right* were undergoing a refit in the two Hill's Dry Docks

36 Roath Dock *c*.1937 with Spiller's recently opened mills in the background

Trade and Industry

37 James Keir (1839-1921), the founder of the Cardiff jewellers' and watchmakers' business outside his shop at 38 Castle Arcade, *c.*1900. The business descended to his son Fred and his grandson Norman, but the shop was moved after the Second World War to 8 Royal Arcade. James Keir Ltd still has an office at 35 St. Mary Street

Railway, Commercial and Family
Temperance Hotel

(Opposite G.W.R. Station).

3 minutes from the General Post Office,
and in Centre of Town.

Commodious Commercial,
Coffee & Smoke Rooms.

Nat. Tel. OIOB.
Telegrams, "Railway Hotel."

A. A. BRYAN,
Proprietor.

38 The *Railway Hotel* in Saunders Road, *c*.1905. By the 1920s the name had been changed
to the *Railway Station Hotel* (probably to avoid confusion with the nearby *South Wales
Railway Hotel* on West Canal Wharf). From 1954 until 1980 it was the *Merchant Navy Hotel*
and then it became *Brownhill's Hotel*. It has recently been re-opened as the *Station Hotel*.
This advertisement appeared in Ed. J. Burrow's 1906 *Guide to Cardiff*

39/40 Two popular old Cardiff pubs provide the backgrounds to these groups. *Above* Local fruiterers proudly display the prizes for their annual sports in 1911. The *Oxford* faced David Morgan's store in the Hayes and was demolished *c*.1961 for the building of Oxford House; *below* Cardiff Ramblers Cycling Club *c*.1908 made the *Clifton*, on the corner of Clifton Street and Broadway, their headquarters

Fresh Fish Arrives Daily at Cardiff

41 Fresh fish was big business in 1932 when this advertisement appeared in *Panoramic Cardiff*, issued by the Cardiff Development Association. Neale & West remained part of the dock scene until the 1960s

STEAM TRAWLER ENTERING CARDIFF DOCKS.

One of Sixteen Modern Vessels Owned by—

NEALE & WEST LIMITED,
Wharf Street :: Cardiff.

Telegrams—" NEALEWEST" CARDIFF.   Telephone—CARDIFF **7260,**

42 Neale & West were always ready to help the local community, like this occasion in the 1930s when they supplied the transport for these Kentucky Minstrels

43 Gitsham's cake shop at 22 Carlisle Street, Splott, in 1908. The family later moved to Llanishen and continued to trade until 1958 when they became part of the new 'Wonderloaf' bakery at Maindy Lane

44 Tom Phillips stands outside his shop on the corner of Cowbridge Road and Aldsworth Road. For many years it was the 'first and last' on the western boundary of the city. Established in 1898 by Tom's father it was a popular 'fags and paper' call for hundreds of workers at the nearby Ely Paper Mills. The business closed in 1979 and Tom, now in his 80s, lives with his wife in Furness Close, Ely

45 Meat roasting on a spit under the watchful eye of the chef made a mouth-watering trade card for the *Old Arcade*, Church Street, in the 1930s

46 Who remembers the *Royal Oak* in Canton? It was situated at 233 Cowbridge Road during the First World War, when this was taken. It closed soon afterwards and the premises were later used at different times by a grocer, as a temperance bar, and by an engineer

47 Staff employed by Collins, the Albany Road drapers, *c.*1922. In the centre of the front row is the manager, Leonard Collins, son of the owner Harry Collins

48 The Kelleher family had a milk business in Splott for many years. Their dairy was on the corner of Swansea Street and Pontypridd Street. Here Eddie Kelleher is standing by his milk float in Portmanmoor Road in the late 1950s

EJM PLATING—THE STORY BEHIND THE NAME

When H. M. Prickett bought E. J. Morgan's plating business in Charles Street in 1930 for £100 a stipulation of the sale, made by the owner's widow, was that his initials—EJM—should be retained in the title of the new company as a tribute to her late husband's memory. Thus it became EJM Plating Ltd, and in 1935 the present factory was built on Newport Road, almost opposite the then Cardiff power station. Fitted with the latest equipment it was the largest out-plating works in Wales at that time undertaking all kinds of chromium and electro plating work.

The first chairman of EJM was H. C. Prickett, one-time owner of the *Moira* hotel in Adamsdown, and the *Griffin* in St. Mary Street who was a city councillor for the Adamsdown ward and, more surprisingly, world speed cycling champion, a title won in France prior to the First World War.

EJM is presently run by J. M. Prickett, the owner's son, who has presided over the firm's expansion since 1950 and was responsible for adding a first floor to the original building in 1965.

49 *Opposite, above* This is how the EJM factory looked, with an enclosed forecourt, railings topping a boundary wall, and double gates, when the adjoining GPO building was constructed in 1938

50 *Opposite, below* EJM's work-force in 1960

51 *Below* A section of the plating shop showing recessed vats

52/53 The name Dale Forty is synonymous with pianos. They occupied spacious premises on the corner of the Castle Arcade and High Street throughout the 1920s, 30s and during the Second World War. By the 1950s they had moved to Premier Buildings in St. John Street and recognising changing fashion were offering a wide variety of musical instruments, radios, television and electrical goods; but this was short-lived and by *c.*1952 the business had folded. Our photographs show *above* staff enjoying an outing—with luxury coach supplied by E. R. Forse of Kingsway—in 1947; and *below* workshop staff on a P. & A. Campbell cruise to Weston-super-Mare in the same year. The donor, Alf Townsend (in cap) is seated third right, and next to him, right, is Horace Gamlin who now runs his own successful musical instrument business in St. Mary Street. The two were apprentice tuners with Dale Forty

Transport

General Station, G.W.R. (2) Cardiff.

54/55 The General Station in the late 1920s before reconstruction. No. 1 departure 'up' platform is now No. 2; the excavation of the station approach allowed a bay to be converted into the present No. 1. Visible between the lines are gas supply hoses for the surviving gaslit coaches and dining car kitchens

G.W.R. General Station (1) Cardiff.

THE BRITISH OXYGEN Co LTD

THE BRITISH OXYGEN Co LTD
EAST MOORS, CARDIFF.
TELEPHONE No 786.

SPEED M.P.H 5.

56/57 Two 'vintage' road haulage vehicles owned by British Oxygen in their early years at East Moors. *Opposite* Driver Harry Burrows *left* and Steersman Ted Bellamy stand by their Aveling & Porter steam wagon (speed 5 mph) outside BO works in 1913; *below* Arthur Day and W. Harcom (donor's father, *standing right*) with their solid tyre Daimler 3 ton (1923 registered) petrol lorry in 1932

58 Open tourer which no doubt was the 'last word' when this advertising photograph was taken in the Civic Centre in the late 1920s

59 Queen Street in 1910. The single-deck tram was operating on the No. 1 route—Monument-Whitchurch Road via Cathays and had just turned out of Windsor Place. Practically all the buildings on the left have gone. Calders survived until March 1987 when the section *left foreground* was demolished for the Queensgate development

60 Tramline renewal in Bute Road *c.*1922. A temporary loop line and points have been installed on ballast *left* while a pointsman stands beside a pile of recently excavated wood blocks. Not surprisingly there is a build-up of trams at Pier Head. We now have traffic lights at this junction where the new Hemingway Road leads to Atlantic Wharf

61 Now one of the city's busiest junctions, traffic was comparatively light in 1939, the tram driver could safely alight and manually change the points from Albany Road tracks to Crwys Road tracks. There has been little change in the facades but many of the shops—Argyll Stores for example—have gone and been replaced by other trades

62 A nostalgic moment as the last tram, suitably decorated, made its way down Whitchurch Road to St. Mary Street on 20 February 1950.
The wording on both sides of the car read:

> To all of you old timers—and you still in your teens,
> Who drove with me through peace and war—packed in just like sardines,
> I'd like to thank you one and all for the patience you have shown,
> And say Farewell to the Finest Folk, that a tram has ever known.
>
> Goodbye my friends, this is the end, I've travelled miles and miles
> And watched your faces through the years show anger, tears and smiles.
> Although you've criticised my looks—and said I was too slow
> I got you there and brought you back through rain and sleet and snow.

Sport and Entertainment

63 Two Welsh International colleagues meet at Ninian Park as Trevor Ford shakes hands with Swansea Town's Ivor Allchurch before the start of the 1956 Welsh Cup Final watched by 37,000— still a record for the competition. The referee is B. Mervyn Griffiths of Newport who had been in charge of the 1953 Blackpool v Bolton 'Stanley Matthews' F.A. Cup Final

Swansea-born Trevor Ford was a colourful personality in Cardiff City's First Division side of the mid-1950s. A controversial figure through his frequent brushes with authority at his various clubs, he was already well-known to City followers from his regular appearances with Wales before his arrival at Cardiff from Sunderland in November 1953 for a Football League record fee of £30,000. It was later revealed by Sir Herbert Merrett that, as City's Chairman, he did not agree with the transfer of Ford and refused to sign the cheque!

Trevor had been a Welsh Schools' international, and first came to senior attention in Swansea Town's wartime team. In January 1947 he asked for a transfer after falling out with the Club's directors over training arrangements, and he then joined Aston Villa.

His all-action style, in the days when goalkeepers could be shoulder-charged whilst in possession of the ball, brought him many goals and he was a popular figure with the Villa Park fans before going to Sunderland in October 1950.

Then came his return to Wales just over three years later, and when he ran out at Ninian Park on 12 December 1953 for his Cardiff City home debut against Middlesbrough, the 30,000 crowd sang 'We'll keep a welcome in the hillsides'.

Trevor's clashes with authority were almost as frequent as those with opposition goalkeepers . . . on one occasion, City had to find a replacement shortly before kick-off in a home

BBC Radio Wales football commentator
RICHARD SHEPHERD
profiles
Ninian Park fifties favourite
TREVOR FORD

game with Birmingham City after manager Trevor Morris had told Ford that he would be returning to the team after injury at inside-forward instead of his usual centre-forward position. In typical fashion, Trevor refused!

He then found himself in trouble with the Football League over making allegations about illegal payments made by clubs to players in his book *I lead the attack*, and he was suspended a few months after the start of the 1956-57 season. His days at Ninian Park were clearly numbered, with young Gerry Hitchens proving a promising replacement in City's forward line, and in March 1957 Trevor moved to Dutch club PSV Eindhoven where he spent three successful years.

He eventually returned in the summer of 1960 to join Newport County, but injury restricted his appearances and later that season he joined Southern League Romford with whom he finished his playing career.

Because of the War, Trevor did not make his peacetime League debut until the age of 23, but went on to score 174 goals in 349 League appearances as well as more in various Cup appearances. He made 38 appearances for Wales between 1946 and 1956, scoring 23 goals, and that was at a time when Welsh matches were mainly against the three other Home Countries each season, games against foreign opposition being comparatively rare.

In latter years, he was in the motor trade in Swansea where he still lives, and he remains one of the most colourful characters of post-war Welsh football.

64 Trevor Ford's arrival in December 1953 was the start of a somewhat controversial three and a half years at Ninian Park

65 Trevor Ford was a familiar figure at Ninian Park before he joined Cardiff City in 1953. Here he is in action for Wales against England at Cardiff during October 1951 as he challenges Wolves goalkeeper Bert Williams

66 The 30,000 crowd which saw his home debut against Middlesbrough on 12 December 1953 sang 'We'll keep a welcome in the hillsides' when he came on to the pitch. Trevor *second from left* is shown here heading the only goal of the game

67 Trevor receives the Welsh Cup after City's 3-2 victory over Swansea from F.A. of Wales President Milwyn Jenkins

68 Celebrations in the City dressing-room after the match with some well-known Ninian Park names. *Back, from left* Alan Harrington, Graham Vearncombe, Gerry Hitchens. *Front, from left* Ron Stitfall, Derrick Sullivan, Danny Malloy, Johnny McSeveney, Colin Baker, Brian Walsh, Trevor Ford

69 Charging goalkeepers was a feature of Trevor's game. But in the 1956 Welsh Cup Final, Swansea's Johnny King was broad enough to withstand it. Watching are Swansea's Arthur Willis and Trevor's eventual successor in City's line-up, Gerry Hitchens

70 The start of Trevor's last season with Cardiff City and this was the first team line-up for the pre-season public practice match against the reserves in August 1956. *Back, from left* Ron Stitfall, Colin Baker, Graham Vearncombe, Danny Malloy, Alan Harrington, Derrick Sullivan; *front, from left* Brian Walsh, Cliff Nugent, Trevor Ford, Gerry Hitchens, Johnny McSeveney

71/72 There was no thought of aggravation from these innocents as they waited for the action at Ninian Park. *Above* A section of the crowd at the City v Treharris Welsh League game on 17 September 1912; *below* Territorial sports day in 1913—with straw boaters much in evidence

73 Thrill of a lifetime for Ernie Curtis as King George V is introduced to the Cardiff City team before the 1927 FA Cup Final. *Left to right* Fred Keenor, Len Davies, Ernie Curtis, Tom Sloan, Billy Hardy, Sammy Irving, Hughie Ferguson and Jimmy Nelson

74 Sixty-two years later and Ernie, sprightly as ever, poses outside his Whitchurch home with *Cardiff Yesterday* author Stewart Williams

75 This is how Wembley Stadium, packed with 90,000 fans, appeared to 19-year-old Ernie Curtis on that historic day in April 1927 when City won the Cup

76 After the game the team required a police escort to get them back to their coach. Fred Keenor, cigarette in mouth, is followed by Jimmy Nelson and Len Davies

77   Severn Road Boys' School soccer team, winners of the Cardiff Schools' Shield, 1900-01. First left in the second row is Jim Keir (donor's father). The tall master standing behind him is John Amos who taught for 40 years at the school. He married Jim's sister Maud Keir

78   Severn Road School soccer team, 1958

79 Wood Street School soccer XI, 1936. The sports master, Mr Walbrook, later played a big part in Cardiff Boys' football

80 Clare Road FC, Sunday League First Division champions and winners of the John Snook Cup, 1926-27

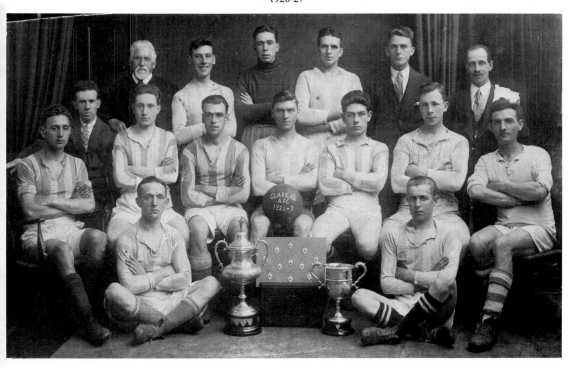

81   Splott Amateurs soccer team in the late 1920s

82   Grange Stars, First Division champions, Cardiff & District League, 1931-32

83 CWS Wheatsheaf soccer team playing in the First Division of the Cardiff & District League, 1922-23 season. The name was derived from the original CWS trade mark

84 National Fire Service soccer XI, 1944

85 A long-standing and eagerly anticipated annual soccer match was that between staff employed by bookselling rivals W. H. Smith and Wymans. The donor, Bert Street, is third from the right in the back row of this Wymans team taken at Llandaff Fields in 1937. Now living in Paignton, he retired in 1981 having worked for Wymans for 48 years

86 Rumney Athletic FC, 1956. Second left in the back row is Bill Barrett

87/88   Canton High School rugby teams. *Above* 'School House' senior XV, season 1949-50; *below* the First XV season 1950-51. The school was a valuable nursery for sporting talent and several boys later distinguished themselves in top-class rugby

89/90 Mackintosh Football Club groups. *Above* The 1894-95 XV. Captain is A. L. Dutton; *below* 1895-96 was a splendid season. The team won the Cardiff & District Football Union league shield. Their record was impressive—played 27, won 23, drew 4; points for, 239, against, 10. Captain is J. Gale

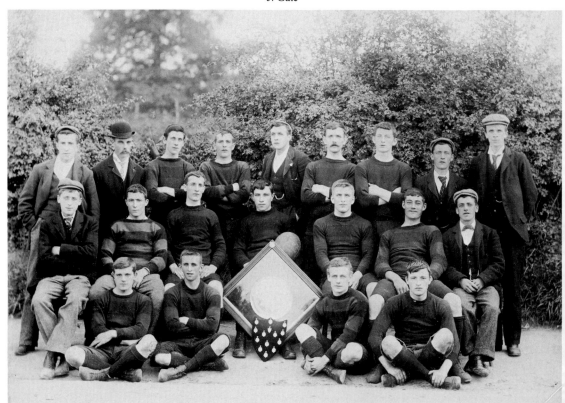

91 St. Mary's, Canton, rugby XV pose with Father Rimmer in 1951

92 Llandaff Technical College rugby team, 1965

93 Spiller's Athletic Club rugby XV, *c.*1932

94 W. J. Rees, Chairman of Cardiff & District Darts League, presenting a cheque to the Lord Mayor (Alderman W. R. Wills) in aid of the Lord Mayor's Distress Fund, on 2 February 1946. Also in the picture, *left to right*, are L. Rees (Vice Chairman), R. V. Coles (Treasurer) and P. Lewis (Secretary)

95 Canton High School 'School House' team competing in the Upper School Relay at the 1949 sports. *Left to right*: Ron Burge, E. Roberts, D. Hurford, Bryan Snaith

96 Canton High School rowing team, 1951

97 St. Saviour's Juvenile Gymnastic Team, winners of the Welsh Juvenile Championship, 1908-09. The hon. instructor (with shield) is P. A. Baker, while the donor's father, Frederick Ronicle, is first left, seated

98 Members of the Plymouth Boxing Club, Earl Lane, Grangetown, in April 1933. *Back row, left to right* Arthur Escott, Albert Welch (Snr.), Nick Gould; *front row* Norman Maplestone, Jackie Pottinger and Albert Welch (Jnr.)

99   Llanishen Hockey Club, season 1911-12. Captain (in pads) is G. H. Maskell

100   Old Monktonians Tennis Club at Victoria Park in 1956

WHITE CITY SPEEDWAY
SLOPER ROAD. CARDIFF

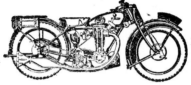

MATCHLESS SPORTS MODEL.

I WILL help you to select your Motor Cycle or Light Car, give you incomparable After Sales Service and, if desired, assist you with a generous Easy Payment System. I will also take your present mount, allowing you market value.

AGENT FOR

A.J.S.	Royal Enfield	Also Austin
Matchless	Scott	Morris and
New Imperial	Triumph and	Triumph
Norton	Velocette	Light Cars

ALEXTHOM

201 CITY ROAD CARDIFF.   **261 CORPORATION RD NEWPORT**

OFFICIAL PROGRAMME
Wednesday, 17th April, 1929
7.30.

6D.

101/102   Now a distant memory, the 'dirt track' in Sloper Road provided thrills and spills galore for sports fans sixty years ago. The course, from start to finish, measured 1633 yards and all races were 'for four laps and for machines with engines no exceeding 500cc'....

. . . Local riders were R. H. 'Whirlwind' Baker, J. H. 'Lightning' Luke, F. C. 'Hurricane' Hampson and C. F. 'Champ' Upham whose daring deeds are legendary. Away from the smoke and the cinders the Capitol was about to introduce 'talkies'. This was 'sport and entertainment' in 1929

THE MARCH OF MELINGRIFFITH

For sheer breadth of musical experience Melingriffith stands head and shoulders above other bands in the Principality. Few can match their record—over 120 broadcasts, more than 1200 concerts in all parts of the country, playing under such distinguished conductors as Sir Adrian Boult, Sir Malcolm Sargent and Sir Arthur Bliss, TV appearances, and five LP records. They have played before King George V, the Prince of Wales, Princess Margaret, Princess Marina, Lady Mountbatten, and various Ministers of State; they were present at the unveiling of the Welsh National War Memorial in Alexandra Gardens in June 1928, and headed two companies of Welsh Guards on recruiting parades through the centre of Cardiff in the early 1940s after the fall of Dunkirk. In peacetime the band played at the opening of the Abbey and Trostre steel-works, the Welsh Industries Fair in London, and scores of other prestigious events. On no less than eleven occasions the band has performed at the National Brass Band Championships at the Albert Hall, and they are four time winners at the Royal National Eisteddfod. Not surprisingly they have a long and colourful history. Founded originally in 1798 as a drum and fife band, they became a brass band in 1850. In 1906 they were the Whitchurch Brass Band, but seven years later this was changed to the Melingriffith Volunteer and Cadet Corps Band. With the firm's patronage a further change to the Melingriffith Works Band came in 1941, and this lasted until their take-over by Excelsior Ropes in 1965. But since 1973 they have been proud to be known once again as the Melingriffith Band. And no doubt they will continue to gather honours and delight audiences with their splendid playing for many years to come.

103 The present Melingriffith Band grew out of earlier combinations including the Whitchurch Brass Band, seen here in September 1908 with their conductor J. Chivers

104/105 Melingriffith Works Band playing on the historic day in June 1948 when the Marquess of Bute handed over Cardiff Castle to the city—one of many prestigious engagements entrusted to them

106 Melingriffith Works Band at the Royal National Eisteddfod at Caerphilly in 1950. The conductor is Tom Powell whose influence over more than 40 years played a big part in the band's success

107 The band soon after the take-over by Excelsior Ropes in 1965

108 GKB Steel Works Home Guard band, *c.*1942, on parade outside the City Hall

109 St. Alban's silver band, 1947

WALDINI
Cardiff's
Mr. Music

110/111 Call it flair, talent, personality . . . Waldini (Wally Bishop) possessed it in ample measure. The popular Cardiff-born cellist formed his first gypsy band in the early 1930s giving work to musicians who found themselves on the show business scrap-heap as the 'talkies' drew the crowds from the live theatre to the cinema. Throughout the 30s Waldini brightened the entertainment scene with his colourful shows playing regular open-air concerts at Roath Park and Sunday concerts at the Park Hall. During the Second World War the band travelled many thousands of miles entertaining the troops, bringing light relief and uplifting spirits in those dark days. Waldini resumed his musical career after the war and played summer shows at several South Coast resorts before becoming a 'regular' at Happy Valley, Llandudno. He died in 1966 but will always be remembered as Cardiff's 'Mister Music'
Inset: Accordions were always featured in Waldini's band. Soloist 'Elaine' appeared with him in hundreds of concerts

112/113/114 In the 1920s and 30s—and certainly during the Second World War—old-time and modern ballroom dancing was probably the most popular recreational activity enjoyed by young Cardiffians. Whether in the Assembly Rooms at City Hall, the big hotels or the scores of modest halls that flourished in all parts of the city, dance music supplied the infectious rhythm that brought couples together on the dance floor. A prominent personality of this period was Madame Hilda Passmore, a music teacher from Splott, who is seen with her Apollo Dance Band *opposite*, at an old-time dance in the City Hall during the late 1920s. Her life was devoted to music and at one time she worked in Woolworth's in Queen Street playing popular pieces from sheet music on the piano in much the same way as records and tapes are demonstrated today. By 1947 Madame Passmore was playing in the Premier dance hall in Queen Street Arcade *below*, with a band which included Tom Cox of Christina Street on drums whose twin sons followed their father into show business as a tap dancing double act. They went on to find fame in cabaret and on TV and the stage, changing their name from the Tornado Twins *right*, to the Cox Twins

TORNADO TWINS

115 An echo of those far-off days of the 1920s and 30s when concert parties like this one entertained us in Roath Park

116 Hilda Banwell and her accordion band, seen here in 1940, gave liberally of their time and talent to entertain members of the forces and munition workers during the Second World War. An accomplished music teacher, Miss Banwell put hundreds of Cardiff youngsters through their piano accordion paces

117 The Snowflakes juvenile choir, First Prize winners at the National Eisteddfod held at Mountain Ash in 1946

118 The Curran Choral Society outside the National Museum of Wales *c*.1942. During the Second World War they gave numerous concerts in the city and won (as here) many Inter-Factory Eisteddfodau. Holding the cup is their conductor, Wyndham Jones, with on his left Eugene Curran

119   Cardiff Municipal Operatic Society's production of 'Rose Marie' at the New Theatre in 1960

120   Cardiff Girls' Choir was started by Edward Charles in 1947 and gave hundreds of concerts at home and abroad during its 40 years existence. Here the choir was about to set out for Coventry in 1970 where they entertained the local Welsh Society with a concert in the Cathedral

121/122 Madame Elvira Hunt's ladies' choir enjoy a privileged position in Cardiff's musical history. For over 50 years their singing gave pleasure to thousands and many deserving charities benefited from their activities. *Above* The choir at a concert in the 1950s; *below* with special guests George Thomas MP and his mother at the annual dinner held at the *Grand Hotel* in the early 1970s. Madame Hunt died in 1977 aged 79

Religion, Education and Public Service

123/124 Ely Gospel Hall was officially opened *above* in 1930 when the new housing estate was being developed. It soon attracted a large following and by 1935 an extension was necessary *below*

125/126 *Opposite* By 1951 when these photographs were taken Ely Gospel Hall had become an important and much-loved influence on Sabbath life in the locality

127 St. Saviour's, Splott, 'Guild of Nazareth', *c*.1925

128 Young strewers from St. Peter's School in the 1952 Corpus Christi procession

129 The Church of St. John the Evangelist in Canton was designed by eminent architect John Prichard. Construction started in 1854 but work was not finally completed until 1902. Sited on an elliptical island, it is a striking building and according to architectural writer John Hilling 'the most completely successful of Prichard's Cardiff churches'

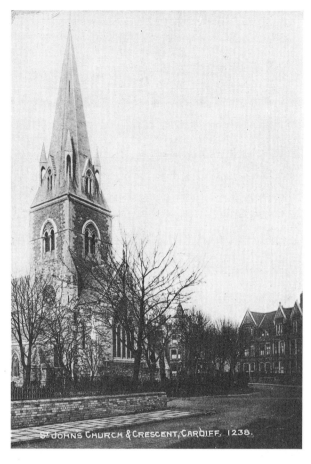

130 'Christ is the Answer' campaign held at Cory Hall in 1953-54. The speaker was Stephen Olford, the chairman Rev. Glyn Owen (minister of Heath Presbyterian Church) and the campaign was organised by Norman J. Rich

131 Charlie Passmore *right* spent many hours building this roundabout for the children of Bridgend Street Mission, Splott, to enjoy at their Whitsun Treats. This was taken at St. Mellons in 1926

132 Canton Salvation Army 'Home League' outing to Symonds Yat in 1930

133 A young Major Tasker Watkins, VC (now Lord Justice Sir Tasker Watkins, QC) after
addressing members of Roath Park Congregational Church Literary Society in 1949

134 Roath Park Congregational Church Youth Club's production of 'The Housemaster' staged in
1954. During the 1940s and 50s the club had a membership of over 100 youngsters

135 Roath Park Congregational (now United Reform Church) Youth Club won this challenge cup at the Cardiff & District Association of Youth Clubs' annual eisteddfod. Myra Harris is receiving the trophy from boxing 'giant' Jack Peterson at the Central Boys' Club in 1954

136 St. Mary's, Canton, Youth Club staged this Christmas pantomime in 1951. Vincent Kane, the broadcaster and journalist, is fifth from left in the second row

137   Pupils of St. Illtyd's College taken at the college playing fields at Blackweir, *c*.1929

138   Fourth formers, Howard Gardens High School, 1935-36

139/140 Many of the 120 or so Canton High pupils in this double-page spread of groups have upheld the school's fine academic reputation by making careers for themselves in the city and further afield. *Above* Third formers in 1947-48; *below* fourth formers in the following year

141/142 *Above* Canton High School fifth formers in 1949-50 with their teacher S. Crammer who was
featured in volume 18; *below* a fine body of sixth formers from 1950-51

143 Rumney Board School and School House in Wentloog Road, *c*.1905. It was replaced by Rumney Central School built by Monmouthshire County Council a few years before Rumney came into the city in 1938

144 Norman J. Rich (in white shirt) sent us this Severn Road 'Peace Year' school group. After spending his working life in local government at the City Hall, Norman has retired to the West Country. He was responsible for the establishment of Ely Gospel Hall (featured in this volume)

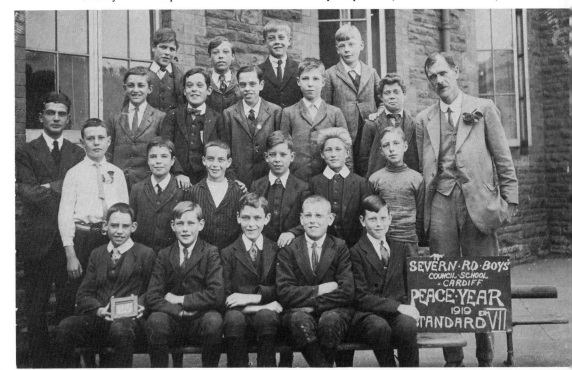

145 Teaching staff at Radnor Road Boys' School in 1930

146 Pupils at Radnor Road Boys' School, 1930

147/148 Infants at Radnor Road School, Canton, in the 1920s and 30s. The 1927 class *above* had fewer smiles for the photographer than their 1938 counterparts *below* who seemed to enjoy the break from lessons

RADNOR Rᵈ
INFANTS

149/150 Junior classes at Radnor Road School in the 1920s and 30s. *Above* This group was taken in 1929; *below* two years later and it was still 'all smiles'

151 Pupils of Radnor Road School, *c.*1937. The teacher is Hubert Jones

152 Class 4, Radnor Road Infants' School, July 1939

RADNOR R^D
INFANTS

153   Pupils of Radnor Road Infants' School, 1940

154   Empire Day celebrations at Radnor Road Girls' School, 1946

155 Radnor Road infants, 1924

156 Pupils at Fairwater Junior School, *c.*1957. The teacher is Howard Spriggs

157/158   In common with most other schools in Cardiff, Fairwater Infants' marked Coronation Year in 1953 with a Fancy Dress Competition. After much deliberation the three seen below were adjudged the winners

159/160   This is diamond jubilee year for Windsor Clive School in Ely which opened its doors to pupils in 1929. *Above* Standard 4a seen in June 1938. The donor, Tom Paul (fifth from left in the back row) recalls that the boys dressed in white shirts had been taking part in country dancing for which they paid 6d a week to cover the cost of the radiogram and records. *Below* In August 1940 the Second World War was in everybody's thoughts which explains the flying helmets in the back row!

161 Some of these Windsor Clive infants, seen in 1931, probably attended the diamond jubilee celebrations held in 1989. The author, himself a former pupil, was one of the judges at a fancy dress party held on 18 January and also attended a party on 1 February when infants and teachers entertained ex-pupils to tea

162 One of the highlights of 1959 for these pupils of Rhiwbina County Primary School was a visit to the Houses of Parliament where the late Raymond Gower, MP gave them a conducted tour

163 These young scholars, including the donor Brian Edwards, extreme right in the middle row, had something to smile about!

164 Reception class at Lansdowne Infants' School, 1948

165   Pupils at St. Peter's Girls' School, *c*.1926

166   Pupils at St. Patrick's Mixed School, Grangetown, 1932

167 Celebrating St. David's Day at Kitchener Infants' School, 1953

168 One or two shy daffodils in this group of Kitchener infants taken on St David's Day, 1958

169 Standard 3, Kitchener School, 1962-63

170 Infants' class at Adamsdown School, 1924

171 Pupils at Albany Road Boys' School, 1905. The school was formally opened on 2 November 1887 by Sir Morgan Morgan, Mayor of Cardiff. On 7 November the children were admitted and by the end of the first week there were 138 girls and 154 boys on roll

172 Pupils at Roath Park Infants' School in 1940

173 Standard 4a, Moorland Road School, 1932

174 Pupils of Grangetown National School, 1927

175 Cardiff Corporation tradesmen taking a breather in between dismantling the old Ely Racecourse grandstand in 1947. It was resited on the recreation ground

176 Upper Splott (Carlisle Street) Civil Defence Unit, *c*.1942

177/178 Members of the National Fire Service stationed at Insole Court, Llandaff (which was renamed Llandaff Court in May 1946) seen here in the early 1940s. These volunteers and thousands like them performed heroically during the Second World War when Hitler's Luftwaffe tried to blitz us into submission

179/180 When the *Terra Nova* left Cardiff Docks at the start of her voyage to the Antarctic on 15 June 1910 she carried on board a flag presented to Captain Scott by the 4th Cardiff (St. Andrews) Boy Scouts. The brave attempt to reach the South Pole ended in tragedy, but the flag survived and was returned to Scoutmaster T. W. Harvey by Lt. Evans on board the *Terra Nova* when she arrived back in Cardiff in June 1913

181/182 The historic flag continued to enjoy a charmed life. When the 4th Cardiff Scout headquarters in Wyeverne Road, Cathays, were flattened by a parachute mine on 29 April 1941 the flag was rescued intact from the rubble

183/184 Known as 'The Lord Mayor's Own' the 14th Cardiff Scout Troop were in their day the elite of the movement. *Below* Posing with the Lord Mayor, Alderman R. G. Hill-Snook, outside the National Museum of Wales in 1930

185 St. Stephen's Scouts in camp at Rhiwbina, *c*.1934. Fifth from right standing is Bill Barrett, recently retired headmaster of Gladstone Junior School and a familiar name to *Cardiff Yesterday* readers

186 65th Cardiff Cubs (Grand Avenue Congregational Church) snapped in the old Welfare Hall, Ely, in 1938

187 13th Cardiff Guides 25th reunion at Grand Avenue Congregational Church, Ely, in 1958

188 53rd Cardiff (Hope Baptist) Girl Guides with their captain, Irene Atkins, in the early 1950s

14TH CARDIFF COY THE BOYS BRIGADE, MAY 1915

189 Against the background of the First World War these lads show extra special pride in their uniforms as they pose with cup and shield, tokens of their proficiency

190 Memorial Hall, Canton, Girls' Brigade with their captain, Mrs Howell Williams, at the Civic Centre in 1935

191 Members of the Grangetown Bridges Committee (including the Mayor, Alderman David Jones) inspecting construction work on Grangetown Bridge on 31 May 1889

192 Labour Exchange staff outside their Paradise Place offices in the late 1930s

Memorable Events

193 'VE' party group in Redlaver Street, Grangetown, May 1945

194 'VE' celebrations in Windway Road, Canton, May 1945

195 Residents of Oakley Street, Grangetown, celebrating the Silver Jubilee of King George V and Queen Mary in 1935. It was Koda Press *right* who printed the author's first modest publishing efforts on jazz and soccer in the 1940s. Along with the *Forge Inn* and the rest of Oakley Street it was demolished in the early 1970s to make way for modern housing

196 These young ladies from Hafod Street and Merches Gardens celebrated the coronation in fine style in 1953

197 Redlaver Street celebrates 'VE' Day with a party for the children in May 1945

198 Cardiff Naturalists' Society (Photographic Section) on a visit to St. Fagan's Castle in September 1912

199 Presentation of the Freedom of the City to the **Rt.** Hon David Lloyd George **MP** on 24 January 1908. It was the first Freedom presentation to take place in the new City Hall. The Lord Mayor was Alderman (later Sir) Illtyd Thomas and Lloyd George is sitting immediately to his right

200/201/202 With banner proudly unfurled the 'Loyal Victoria Lodge' of the Oddfellows march along Frederick Street on August Bank Holiday Monday, 1890

Frederick Street then consisted in the main of working-class housing that had been developed by the Vachell brothers in the 1840s

The route took in Bute Street. Here the procession is passing Edwin Beard's premises on the corner of Maria Street

203/204 Garden parties where the distinguished could mingle together socially were a good way of raising funds for the recently re-named King Edward VII Hospital in the years just before the First World War. It became Cardiff Royal Infirmary in 1923

205 Chief Inspector D. Rankin, Commander of 'D' Division of the City Police based in the Law Courts, died on 3 June 1910. Headed by members of the Watch Committee and followed by the Chief Constable with the other three Divisional Superintendents, the cortege leaves the Law Courts on its way to Cathays Cemetery

206 William Cubitt lived for over 30 years in the distinctively towered Rumney House on Rumney hill which was demolished in the mid-1930s. His daughter's wedding in 1914 was a grand affair enjoyed by the whole village. His coachman for many years was Harry Pacey, seen here in shiny topper

207 Members of Rumney Conservative Club on a visit to Royal Ascot for Gold Cup Day, *c.*1946

208 Members of Riverside Conservative Club outside temporary premises in Pontcanna Street prior to departing on an outing in 1947. Their original home in Neville Street was blitzed during the Second World War and it was not until 1948 that they returned to rebuilt premises

209 Members of Canton, British Railways, staff motor club leaving the General Station in October 1969 for a five-day visit to Germany which included visits to the Mercedes-Benz works at Stuttgart and also to the Daimler-Benz Museum

210 Local historian Bill O'Neill, *third from right*, was runner-up in this 'Golden Years Award' competition held in 1985 when he was 78, to find the Principality's liveliest pensioner. A loyal supporter of *Cardiff Yesterday*, Bill is well-known for his tireless work on behalf of the local elderly care association

211 Christmas Day 1923 and 'fun and games' aboard HMS *Cardiff*. Launched in 1917 this light cruiser made nautical history on 21 November 1918 when, flying the flag of Rear Admiral E. S. Alexander Sinclair, she led the British Fleet to rendezvous with the German Fleet and then led the whole flotilla to anchorage at Inchkeith in the Firth of Forth. The scene is captured in a large painting which hangs in the Lord Mayor's Parlour at City Hall

212 *Craddock Hotel*, Ninian Park Road, 'regulars' looking a touch self-conscious in their party hats as they pose for the camera before setting off on a summer outing in the early 1930s